Tall Tales of the Wild West
(And a Few Short Ones)

A Humorous Collection of Cowboy Poems and Songs

Eric Ode

Meadowbrook Press
Distributed by Simon & Schuster
New York

Library of Congress Cataloging-in-Publication Data

Ode, Eric.
  Tall tales of the wild west (and a few short ones) : a humorous collection of cowboy poems and songs / by Eric Ode ; illustrated by Ben Crane.
      p. cm.
  Summary:"A collection of funny tall tales featuring cowboys, cowgirls, and other characters from the Wild West"—Provided by publisher.
  ISBN 0-88166-524-X (Meadowbrook Press) 1-4169-3677-7 or 978-1-4169-3677-0 (Simon & Schuster)
  1. Cowboys—West (U.S.)—Juvenile poetry. 2. Ranch life—West (U.S.)—Juvenile poetry. 3. Children's poetry, American. 4. American poetry—21st century.
5. Children's songs. I. Crane, Ben, ill. II. Title.
PS3615.D43T35 2007
811'.6—dc22   2006027602

9/07
J
05

Project Director: Bruce Lansky
Coordinating Editor and Copyeditor: Angela Wiechmann
Editorial Assistant and Proofreader: Alicia Ester
Production Manager: Paul Woods
Graphic Design Manager: Tamara Peterson
Illustrations and Cover Art: © 2007 Ben Crane

Published by Meadowbrook Press, 5451 Smetana Drive, Minnetonka, Minnesota 55343

www.meadowbrookpress.com

BOOK TRADE DISTRIBUTION by Simon and Schuster, a division of Simon and Schuster, Inc., 1230 Avenue of the Americas, New York, New York 10020

12 11 10 09 08 07   10 9 8 7 6 5 4 3 2 1

Printed in China

Dedication
With love to Mom and Dad
—Eric

Acknowledgments
Many thanks to the following teachers and their students,
who tested poems and songs for this collection:

Ursula Akridge, Warner Robins, GA
Dawn Carlson, East Elementary, New Richmond, WI
Janelle Edwards, Waverley Memorial/L.C. Skerry Schools, Waverley, NS
Mary Jensen, East Elementary, New Richmond, WI
Cathy Rodrigue, Deer Creek Elementary, Crowley TX
Stephanie Torczon, Media Specialist, New Prague Intermediate School, New Prague, MN

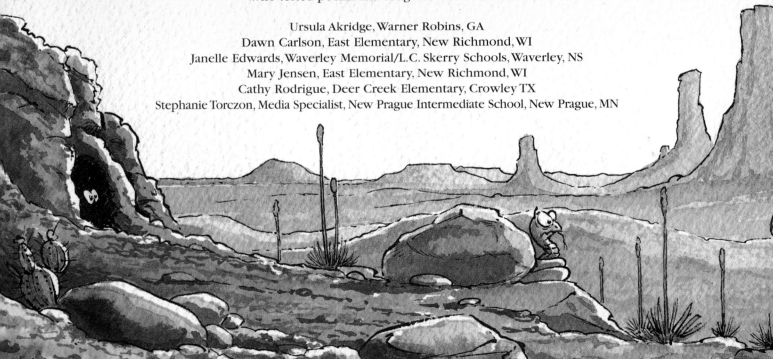

Contents

On Top of My Donkey

(sing to the tune of "On Top of Old Smoky")

On top of my donkey
all covered with fleas,
we stink like a polecat
and old, moldy cheese.

The bears and the panthers
are nothing to fear.
Our smell is so dreadful,
they never come near.

We turn over boulders
to find what's beneath.
The green bugs are tasty,
but stick to our teeth.

We ride through the canyons,
through wind, rain, and frost.
We're bold and courageous
and frequently lost.

So come join our journey.
We do as we please,
just me and my donkey
all covered with fleas.

Horseflies

Flies out west are mighty tough.
They're big and rough and wild.
I swatted one the other day;
it turned around and smiled.

"I've got an awful itch," it said,
"so would you try once more?
But this time slightly to the left
and higher than before."

The Barrel Race

Jessie was the master of the western rodeo.
Her name was known from Texas to the state of Idaho.
She rode her horse from town to town, and everywhere she went,
she proved herself the master of each rodeo event.

She rode the bucking broncos, and she wrestled down the steers.
She roped the calves in record time to whistles, shouts, and cheers.
But one day Jess heard hollering, and following the roar,
she watched a competition she had never seen before.

They called it barrel racing, an event of speed and skill.
And Jessie said, "I've never tried, but I believe I will."
The challenge of this new event was plain enough to see.
The barrels marked the racing track, and there were only three.

So Jessie checked the stirrups as she saddled up her horse,
and soon the two were speeding through that barrel racing course.
The crowd was up and cheering as they rounded barrel one,
and Jessie whooped and gave a shout, "Now this is heaps of fun!"

They rounded barrels two and three. The cheers were loud and steady.
But Jessie thought, "It seems a shame to end this race already.
If I've had this much fun before, I can't remember when."
She spurred her horse and gave a shout, "Let's go around again!"

The crowd was quite bewildered when they saw she wasn't through.
They watched her turn her horse again from barrel one to two.
At barrel three, the people thought she surely must be done,
but once again she circled and went back to barrel one.

The people stared in wonder. They could not believe their eyes.
The minutes turned to hours, and the moon began to rise.
So one by one, they headed home, and soon the crowd was gone.
But through it all, that girl and horse kept racing on and on.

The crowd returned next afternoon to see if Jess was done,
and there she was, still riding hard as if she'd just begun.
But all that time upon the track and racing 'round and 'round
had left a valley six or seven inches in the ground.

By supper time the horse had dug that valley all the deeper.
The floor was nearly eight feet down. The walls were growing steeper.
And still she smiled and still she traveled fast and fancy-free,
but Jessie's dusty cowboy hat was all the folks could see.

Now years have come and years have gone since Jess began that ride.
And no one's seen her since those days, although some folks have tried.
But somewhere near a canyon, if you listen now and then,
perhaps you will hear Jessie shout, "Let's go around again!"

Rusty Rose Takes a Bath

That desperado, Rusty Rose,
he scratched his horse's ear.
He said, "I see you curl your nose
whenever I am near.

"I hate the thought, but I suppose
it's got to be this way.
So up ahead, I'll shed these clothes
and take a bath today."

They came upon a riverbed
beside a ragged tree,
and Rusty said, "Now bow your head
and say a prayer for me."

He grabbed a crusty bar of soap
and stripped down to the skin.
And then without a shred of hope,
poor Rusty stumbled in.

A bullfrog fled without a trace,
a fish came up for air,
as Rusty washed his hands and face,
his legs and feet and hair.

He dried off with a gunnysack
and hung it in the tree.
He climbed aboard his horse's back,
his hat upon his knee.

"We'll leave the soap beside the path,"
said Rusty with a sneer.
"I might just need another bath
when we come back next year."

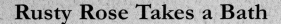

WANTED:

Martin Suds

This dirty bandit stole a tub
and scrambled in to soak and scrub.
Martin Suds, the people say,
made a real clean getaway.

Horseshoes

We love a game of horseshoes at the closing of the day,
but no one dares to start a game when Big Mike wants to play.
He's mighty good at horseshoes, and he simply can't be matched,
'cuz Big Mike likes to throw them while the horse is still attached.

Horse Sense

The deputy looked puzzled, and the sheriff scratched his head.
"I think we've got a problem here," the sheriff slowly said.
"We stood our horses side by side, and now it's sad but true:
I cannot tell which horse is mine and which belongs to you."

"I think I have the answer," said the deputy with pride.
"A saddle's on my horse's back. A rope is at his side."
"I'm sorry, friend," the sheriff said. "That ain't no way to tell.
My horse has got a saddle, too. He's got a rope as well."

"My horse is wearing saddlebags," the deputy explained.
"I've got a hat and blanket there in case it snowed or rained."
"I've got the same," the sheriff said, "and maybe you'll remember
you got yours for your birthday, and I bought mine in September."

The deputy then clapped his hands. "My horse likes sugar beets!"
"But so does mine," the sheriff said. "They're all he ever eats."
"I reckon," said the deputy, "we're gonna have to choose.
It's very near impossible to tell whose horse is whose."

"I've got it!" said the sheriff with a whistle and a holler.
"I've seen them both together, and I think my horse is taller."
He measured up the horses then to see which was the right one.
And sure enough, the spotted horse was bigger than the white one.

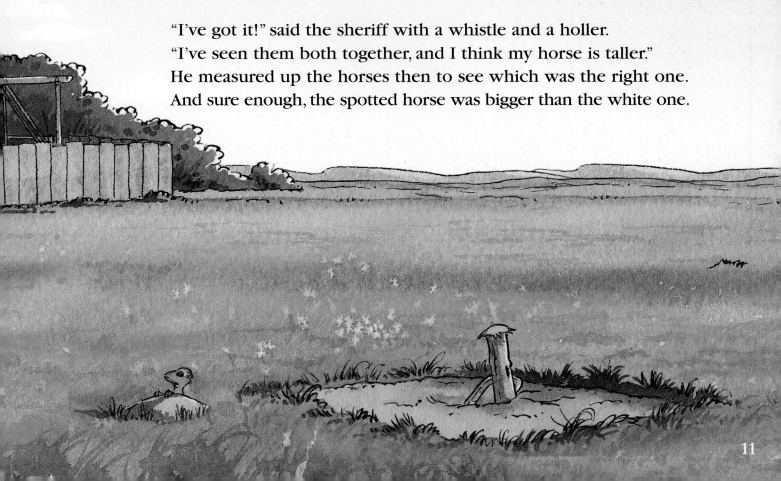

Horseshoe Hannah

(sing to the tune of "Oh, Susanna")

Oh, I rode from Alabama to a hot and dusty land
where I met my Horseshoe Hannah with a six-gun in her hand.
And she said, "This is a holdup!" Oh, her voice was so divine
that I shouted, "Horseshoe Hannah, oh my darlin', please be mine!"

Chorus
Horseshoe Hannah, oh, won't you be my bride?
You can wear your white bandana with your six-gun at your side.

Well, she looked a little puzzled, and she said, "Don't be absurd!
I'm the roughest, toughest outlaw that you've ever seen or heard."
Then she said, "Now put your hands up, and you keep them high above."
And I wept because my Hannah couldn't see we were in love.

Chorus

When she reached into my saddlebags, I kissed her on the cheek.
But she tied me up—I reckon she was too in love to speak.
And I thought about it sadly as I watched my darlin' part.
No, it wasn't just my money—Horseshoe Hannah stole
    my heart.

Chorus

Turkey on the Run

(sing to the tune of "Turkey in the Straw")

Spent the day upon the saddle. I was hungry as a bear.
Put the kettle on the fire, fetched a table and a chair.
Then I stepped out of the cabin, and I took a look around,
and I found myself a turkey who was sleeping on the ground.

Chorus
Turkey on the run. Turkey in the air.
Supper isn't done. I'm hungry as a bear.
It's hard to catch a turkey when you haven't got a gun,
so the kettle's on the fire, but the turkey's on the run.

Well, the turkey heard me coming, and he ran across the sand,
so I followed close behind him with a hatchet in my hand.
Then he jumped into a gulley where the spiny cactus grows,
and I spent a half an hour pulling needles from my nose.

Chorus

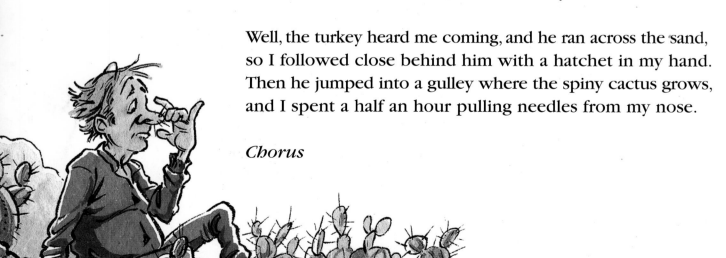

Well, I thought I had the turkey when he flew into a tree,
so I reached into the branches where I reckoned he would be.
But I found I was mistaken when I tried to grab his head.
What I thought had been the turkey was a porcupine instead.

Chorus

Then he swam across a river for to reach the other side.
And I'd like to say I caught him, but at least I'll say I tried.
Well, the water sure was icy and the bird was hard to hold,
so I didn't catch the turkey, but I caught myself a cold.

Chorus

If you're ever on the prairie and you see that silly bird,
you should think about my story. You should take me at my word.
If you're feeling rather hungry and a little underfed,
just forget about the turkey—have a slice of buttered bread.

Chorus

Mulligan Martinson Marley McGraw

The tiniest cowboy the world ever saw
was Mulligan Martinson Marley McGraw.
He bathed in a teacup and rode on a rat
and wore very proudly a mighty small hat.

Now, Mulligan fancied a life on the range,
but townsfolk considered him silly and strange.
They called him a dreamer, a fool, and a clown.
"You're simply too small," said the people in town.

"You can't brand a steer or deliver a calf.
You can't mend a fence," said the folks with a laugh.
They sneered at the way he would yodel and sing.
They scoffed at the lasso he made out of string.

But Mulligan said as he stuck out his chin,
"A winner don't quit, and a quitter don't win.
You say what you will—I don't care about that.
A cowboy is more than the size of his hat."

And so life continued, as life often does,
till early one morning the streets were abuzz.
And people were panicking uphill and down
with news that the prairie dogs moved into town.

They came without warning, three thousand or more,
invading the homes and the general store.
They slipped into socks and the pockets of suits.
They squeezed into boxes and barrels and boots.

They slept under tables. They crept under chairs.
They filled all the benches and stables and stairs.
And no one in town seemed to know how to cope.
Those critters were simply too tiny to rope.

The sheriff then shouted, "We'll seek and we'll search.
We'll clean out the barns and the school and the church.
We'll round up them varmints. We'll get the job done!"
The folks tried their darndest, but caught not a one.

But Mulligan Martinson said with a grin,
"A winner don't quit, and a quitter don't win.
As sure as a hound dog is riddled with fleas,
I'll round up them critters as quick as you please."

The townspeople chuckled but said not a word
as Mulligan left for that prairie dog herd.
His boots in the stirrups, his string at his side,
he guided his rat through the streets far and wide.

He rode through the houses, the bank, and the jail,
and lassoed them dogs by the tip of the tail.
Then one to the next, like the cars of a train,
he built him a seven-mile prairie-dog chain.

The people applauded. They shouted and cheered
as into the sunset that herd disappeared.
But that was the last that the town ever saw
of Mulligan Martinson Marley McGraw.

The folks like to say that he's still on the plains.
He's guiding that herd with his hands on the reins.
He left us a lesson—no doubt about that:
A cowboy is more than the size of his hat.

Her Darling Valentine

(sing to the tune of "Clementine")

In a cabin on the prairie
lived a girl the age of nine.
And the label on her stable
said her horse was Valentine.

Chorus
He's her darling, he's her darling,
  he's her darling Valentine.
Kind and clever friend forever,
  and she calls him Valentine.

'Cross the prairie swept a shadow—
seven bandits in a line.
Fierce and fright'ning, fast as lightning,
come to capture Valentine.

Now the girl yelled out in anger
at the vile and vicious swine.
And she hurried, mad and worried,
to her precious Valentine.

Chorus

Oh, she chased them, and she roped them,
and she wrapped them up in twine.
And she packed them, and she stacked them
on the back of Valentine.

As she rode them to the sheriff,
she was singing soft and fine,
"Here's a lesson: Don't be messin'
with my darling Valentine.

"He's my darling, he's my darling,
  he's my darling Valentine.
Kind and clever, and I'll never leave
  my darling Valentine."

The Great Chili Cook-Off

At the Great Chili Cook-Off of Tenderfoot Valley,
the whole town was gathered—each Tom, Dick, and Sally—
to see who would win and be given the crown
of Chili Bean Princess of Tenderfoot Town.

Now, Millicent Milkweed was graceful and stunning,
and she'd been the winner for seven years running.
She stood near her kettle with beauty and style
and waved to the crowd with a confident smile.

The other contestants expected the worst:
that Millicent's chili would surely be first.
The best they could hope for, as far as they reckoned,
was coming in third or perhaps even second.

A sweet, spicy smell filled the fall afternoon
as bravely they waited with kettle and spoon.
Then in walked a lady quite new to the town,
with sun-speckled freckles of cinnamon brown.

She carried a kettle that gurgled and bubbled
and sheepishly grinned, looking timid and troubled.
Her hair, like a bison's, was woolly and shaggy.
Her apron was rumpled. Her bonnet was baggy.

She set down her kettle on top of the table
and brushed from her fingers the dirt from her stable.
She smoothed out her dress for a moment or two
and pulled out a spoon she had tucked in her shoe.

Then Millicent glared at this strange-looking lady,
who said to her, "Howdy. I'm Isabelle Grady.
I came here as soon as I finished my chores.
I hope I ain't late for this contest of yours."

The judge entered in with a top hat and suit.
He turned to the crowd, and he gave a salute.
He said not a word, but was off like a shot
to see what he'd find in the first chili pot.

This chili belonged to one Bernadette Bly,
who watched as the judge gave her chili a try.
He grunted, and soon without further ado,
he moved down the table to pot number two.

Now, pot number two the judge met with a yawn.
He sniffed and he nibbled, but soon he was gone.
And three, four, and five were each greeted the same.
That judge hurried on just as quick as he came.

But pot number six—that was Millicent's chili.
She smiled at the judge, and he winked back at Millie.
He said as he tasted, "Well, Millicent dear,
that's pretty good chili you've cooked up this year."

"But still," said the judge, "there's no need to be hasty.
There's one kettle left, and it smells rather tasty."
He lowered a spoon into Isabelle's pot
and said to her, "Now then, let's see what you've got."

The judge took a bite, and he blinked and he shivered.
His mouth, it dropped open. His mustache, it quivered.
And long wisps of steam drifted up from his nose
while billows of smoke left his fingers and toes.

And then before anyone there was the wiser,
he flew through the air as if shot from a geyser.
But Isabelle heard as he vanished from sight,
"Now, that pot of chili is just about right!"

The Prospector

Miss Polly May, so we are told,
would spend her seasons panning gold.
She'd grit her teeth and hope and dream
and thrust her pan into the stream,
but what Miss Polly May would find
was nothing like she'd had in mind.
"I feel like such an utter fool,"
she'd tell her gray and shaggy mule.
"I dip my pan. I pull it out.
But all I get are rocks and trout.

Oh, how I dream and how I wish
I'd bring up gold instead of fish."
But one day as she held her pan,
Miss Polly May devised a plan.
She bought a hammer, nails, and wood
and did just what she knew she should.
She built a shop. She made a sign.
And now the people stand in line.
Throughout the west, they're making trips
to Polly's Pan-Fried Fish and Chips.

A Cowboy's Letter to Santa

Dear Santa,

The year is nearly over.
I've been trying to be good.
I've roped and rounded cattle
like a working cowboy would.
I've led them to the pastures,
and I've led them through the plains.
I've crossed them over mountains
in the icy winter rains.

The gifts you brought a year ago,
they certainly are swell.
I like the boots. I like the vest.
I like the hat as well.
The saddle's still as good as new.
I try to keep it clean.
The bridle, bit, and stirrups are
the best I've ever seen.

I'll keep this letter simple.
You're a busy buckaroo.
The gifts you brought a year ago
are mighty fine—it's true.
It's not that I'm complaining.
I was much obliged, of course.
The pogo stick was dandy,
but I *really* need a horse!

The Armadillo

"Hold up just a minute, boys,"
said Sheldon with a shout.
"I think there's something in my boot,
so let me dump it out."

He slipped down from the saddle,
and he sat beneath a willow.
And there inside his cowboy boot
he found an armadillo.

"Well, blow me down!" the cowboy said.
"I knew that things were wrong.
I hope, my friend, you don't intend
to stay there very long."

"I wouldn't dare," the critter said,
"for near as I can tell,
I might survive the crowded fit,
but surely not the smell!"

The Dance

A hard-working cowboy was Chesterton Clyde,
and Anabelle Sue was the horse he would ride.
Together they traveled the hills far and wide,
the cowboy and Anabelle Sue.

Now, late on a Friday they rode into town,
and Chesterton watched as the sun settled down.
Then sweaty and dusty and dirty and brown,
he climbed off of Anabelle Sue.

From off in the distance, a banjo was heard
and joined by a fiddle as sweet as a bird.
So Chesterton followed but said not a word
while leading his Anabelle Sue.

They came to a barn where a mandolin played
and folks in their finest, they spun and they swayed.
The cowpuncher sighed at the soft serenade
along with his Anabelle Sue.

A pretty young lady, so gentle and fair
was dressed up with flowers and bows in her hair.
She smiled very sweetly and blushed at the pair,
that cowboy and Anabelle Sue.

The melody soared with the sounds of romance
as softly she said, "It's a fine night to dance."
She gave to the cowboy a hesitant glance
while petting old Anabelle Sue.

"I reckon it is," answered Chesterton Clyde.
"I ain't danced before, but it's high time I tried."
Then bowing politely, he shuffled inside
and danced with his Anabelle Sue.